D0461435

XTREME JOBS

STUNT PERFORMER

BY S.L. HAMILTON

A&D Xtreme
An imprint of Abdo Publishing | www.abdopublishing.com

Visit us at
www.abdopublishing.com

Printed in the United States of America, North Mankato, Minnesota.
052015
092015

Editor: John Hamilton
Graphic Design: Sue Hamilton
Cover Design: Sue Hamilton
Cover Photo: AP
Interior Photos: Alamy-pgs 8-9, 14-15, 15 (inset), 17, 20-21, 24-25 & 28-29; AP-pgs 1, 4-5, 12-13, 16, 18-19, 23 (inset) & 30-31; Corbis-pgs 2-3, 10-11, 22-23, & 26-27; Glow Images-pg 32; Paramount Pictures-pg 7 (bottom); United Artists-pgs 6 & 7 (top).

Websites
To learn more about Xtreme Jobs, visit booklinks.abdopublishing.com. These links are routinely monitored and updated to provide the most current information available.

Library of Congress Control Number: 2015930965

Cataloging-in-Publication Data

Hamilton, S.L.
   Stunt performer / S.L Hamilton.
      p. cm. -- (Xtreme jobs)
   ISBN 978-1-62403-760-3
   1. Stunt performers--Juvenile literature.   I. Title.
   791.4320--dc23

2015930965

CONTENTS

STUNT PERFORMER

Stunt performers knock on death's door every time they go to work. As long as there have been movies, men and women stunt performers have been in the business of making falls, fights, and chases look spectacular. It's the job of these brave, skilled athletes to perform a film's most dangerous stunts.

XTREME FACT – Stunt work accounts for more than half of all movie-related injuries.

5

HISTORY

Today's stunt performer job took shape with the invention of the motion picture camera in the 1890s. By the 1920s, tough people such as cowboys, construction workers, and soldiers performed death-defying stunts on movie sets. A few actors performed their own stunts.

Actor Buster Keaton risks death in this famous stunt (front view above and side view below) in 1928's **Steamboat Bill, Jr.**

XTREME QUOTE – "I was mad at the time, or I would never have done the thing." –Buster Keaton, referring to letting a 3-ton (2.7 metric ton) house fall while he stands in the open window area.

Stuntman James "Bud" Ekins jumps a motorcycle over a 12-foot (3.7-m) barbed-wire fence in the 1963 movie The Great Escape. *It is one of the most famous stunts in movie history.*

As time passed, stunts became more and more dangerous. Studios wanted to protect their stars. Stunt performers became vital to movie production.

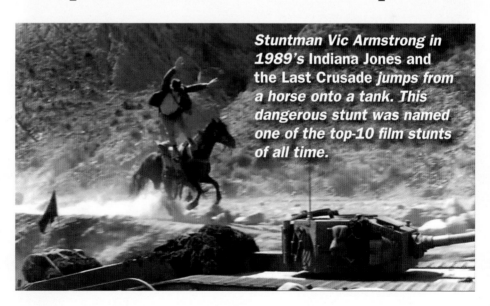

Stuntman Vic Armstrong in 1989's Indiana Jones and the Last Crusade *jumps from a horse onto a tank. This dangerous stunt was named one of the top-10 film stunts of all time.*

GAGS

Stunt performers call their dangerous work "gags." A motorcycle through a window is a gag. A high fall is a gag. And so on. Some stunt professionals have experience in nearly every type of movie gag. Others are experts at specific gags. Stunt performers are hired to work on a movie based on their athletic skills and how well they work as part of the movie's stunt team. They must also look like the actor for whom they are stunt doubling.

XTREME FACT– To do stunt work for movies and TV, stunt performers are usually members of SAG-AFTRA (Screen Actors Guild-American Federation of Television and Radio Artists). It is a labor union that oversees safety and fair pay.

A stunt performer crashes through a stained-glass window in 2004's Resident Evil: Apocalypse.

PRECISION DRIVING

Making a movie director's idea of a vehicle stunt a reality takes careful planning. Vehicle gags are mapped out by a movie's stunt coordinator. This stunt leader uses toys, storyboards, mathematical measurements, and his or her own experience to find a way to make the stunt work.

10

The stunt driver, or "wheelman," may be part of a multi-vehicle chase sequence, a crash, a slide, a jump, or a rollover. They may have to pass people at high rates of speed. Stunt performers must have perfect timing. People's lives depend on it.

XTREME QUOTE – *"Doing crashes is actually very difficult because it goes against all your instincts. That's why racing drivers don't necessarily make great stunt people, because in stunt work you have to do everything against your better nature and judgement."* –Vic Armstrong, stuntman

Motorcycle gags include everything from wheelies to jumps to hanging from the handlebars. Stunt performers may ride on city streets or off-road on rough paths.

Unlike cars, motorcycles have no metal protecting stunt performers. Stunt performers depend on their own skills, as well as helmets, protective jackets, gloves, and boots to stay safe.

XTREME FACT– When filming a stunt, several cameras are placed at different locations so the action can be captured from many angles at the same time.

Boat stunt drivers are called on to do many different gags, including boat chases, jumps, flips, and water-to-land stunts. Some very dangerous stunts, including those that are performed close to propeller blades, are performed in huge water tanks.

XTREME FACT – In the 1973 James Bond movie Live and Let Die, *the stunt team made 100 practice runs and wrecked 17 boats before they perfected the boat jump from water, across a strip of land, and back into the water–a record distance of 110 feet (34 m).*

HIGH FALLS

Falling from a distance of three stories or more is considered a high fall gag. Stunt performers learn to fall into water, air bags, foam-filled PortaPits, or a collection of cardboard boxes known as box catchers. Stunt performers may also use harnesses, rigs, and vests during falling gags. They must be skilled in different types of falls, such as headers, back falls, and twists.

A student performs a high fall at the International Stunt School in Seattle, Washington.

A harnessed stuntman performs a high fall on the movie set of 2008's G.I. Joe.

XTREME FACT – High falls kill more stunt performers than any other gag. To do a fall safely, they must land flat.

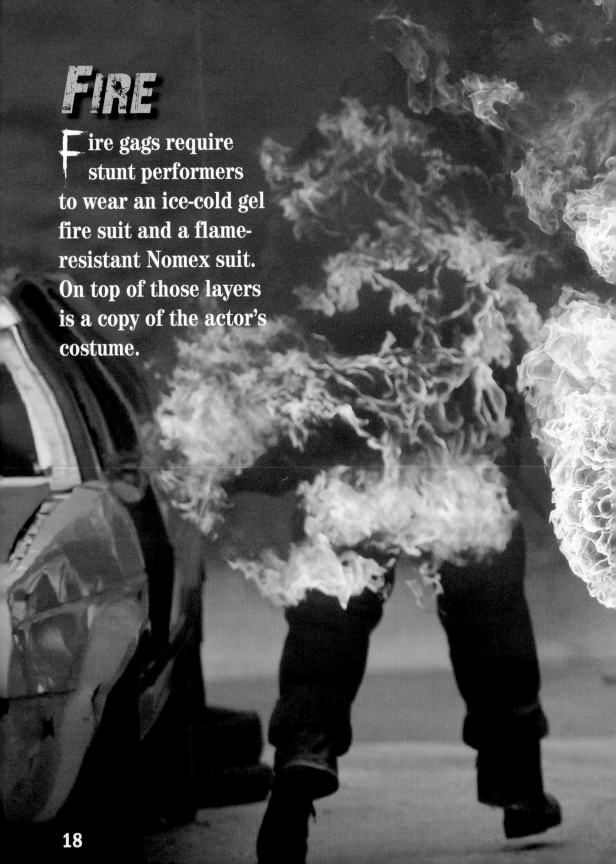

FIRE

Fire gags require stunt performers to wear an ice-cold gel fire suit and a flame-resistant Nomex suit. On top of those layers is a copy of the actor's costume.

To protect exposed flesh from fire, such as the face or hands, stunt performers coat their skin with a special burn gel. However, the gel only works as long as it is wet. Once it dries, it's useless. The stunt has be performed as soon as the gel is in place.

XTREME QUOTE – "Down, down, down!"
–Stunt coordinator, yelling at a burning stunt performer to get on the ground so the stunt crew can put out the fire.

19

CRASHING THROUGH GLASS

Having a stunt performer crash through a window is a common movie gag. Products called breakaway glass or sugar glass are used to protect stunt performers. Breakaway glass is made of a special type of resin. Sugar glass is made of sugar, corn syrup, and water. These products look like glass, but do not break into sharp, dangerous pieces.

XTREME FACT – In early movie-making, a thin layer of ice was sometimes used as breakaway glass. It was much more dangerous than today's products.

EXPLOSIONS

A movie script may call for an actor to run away from an exploding bomb or car. Stunt performers are tossed through the air or jerked back in these dramatic action sequences. The gag usually requires the stunt performer to wear a harness attached to a wire. At the moment of the explosion, the actor is pulled back by the wire. Timing must be perfect for the action to look as though the person is caught in a violent blast. It is an exciting gag that many stunt performers find fun.

XTREME FACT – An air ram catapult may be used to mimic a person being thrown forward in an explosion. The stuntman stands on the platform and at the correct moment, an operator pushes a button to send him through the air to land in an air bag or PortaPit. The stunt crew surrounds the landing area as safety spotters.

PUNCHES

Movie punches are supposed to be close, but not make contact. Sometimes stunt performers really get hit. Whether or not a punch makes contact, it may look fake on film. The stunt coordinator calls that a "miss." What makes a punch "connect," or look real, is often the stunt performer's reaction. If people act like they've been hit, the audience believes it.

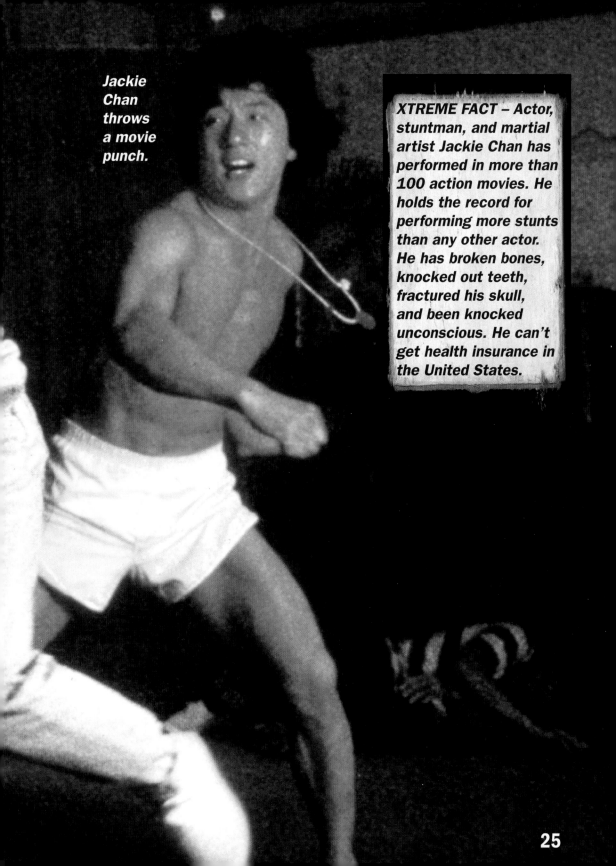

Jackie Chan throws a movie punch.

XTREME FACT – Actor, stuntman, and martial artist Jackie Chan has performed in more than 100 action movies. He holds the record for performing more stunts than any other actor. He has broken bones, knocked out teeth, fractured his skull, and been knocked unconscious. He can't get health insurance in the United States.

JUMPS

Stunt performers must be able to run fast and jump high and far. They learn to absorb the force of a landing by bending their knees. A bad landing can result in a broken ankle or bone. However, a stunt performer will often have to do more than run and jump. This action is often combined with climbing, swinging, vaulting, and rolling. All these skills come with practice.

Actor Taylor Lautner performs his own stunt for the 2015 movie, Tracers.

JOB FACTS

To become a stunt performer requires a high degree of athletic ability and a sense of fearlessness. Some athletes and actors train at stunt schools, such as the International Stunt School in Seattle, Washington.

Stunt performers are paid a minimum of $829 per day as of 2013. They may earn $3,200 if they are paid by the week. Performing dangerous stunts gives them extra money or "bumps" in pay. They are paid this amount every time they do a very difficult stunt, but they hope to do it only once.

XTREME QUOTE – "There's no such thing as a great stunt if there's no danger involved."
–Hal Needham, stuntman

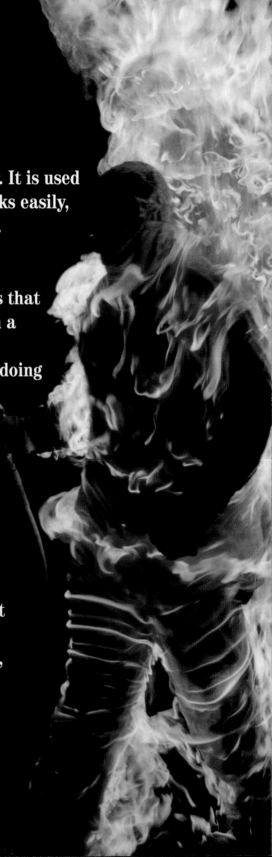

GLOSSARY

BREAKAWAY GLASS
A fake glass made of plastic or sugar. It is used for stunts because it looks real, breaks easily, and does not cut the stunt performer.

CHASE SEQUENCE
A series of many short, intercut shots that combine to make a complete chase in a film. The chase sequence may show a driver being pursued, another driver doing the chasing, a vehicle that crashes, and views inside and outside the vehicles.

NOMEX SUIT
A one-piece suit worn by stunt performers that is made of Nomex, a material with excellent flame resistance. Nomex material does not melt, and the flame resistance cannot be washed out. Nomex suits are also worn by race car drivers, firefighters, and military flight crews. There are also Nomex gloves, balaclavas, hoods, long underwear, shirts, pants, and socks.

PORTAPIT

A foam-filled stunt pad used as a safe landing area for stunt performers when doing a limited-height fall in a confined area. PortaPit pads come in different

PortaPit

sizes, weights, densities of foam, and shape. They are made to be moved around and then anchored in position.

SEQUENCE

A collection of scenes that make up a period of continuous action.

STUNT COORDINATOR

An experienced stunt performer who hires and coordinates all of the stunts in a film, TV, or theater production. The stunt coordinator works with the production's director.

STUNT CREW

A group of stunt performers who work together on a specific production. The stunt crew typically reports to the stunt coordinator.

STUNT DOUBLE

A person who stands in for an actor in a movie in order to perform a dangerous or tricky stunt. Also, another name for a stunt performer.

WHEELMAN

A nickname for a stunt performer driving a car.

INDEX